For Love of Woman

John Saomes

Inspire Point
PUBLISHING

Copyright © John Saomes 2020

www.johnsaomes.com

The right of John Saomes to be identified as the author of this work has been asserted in accordance with the Copyright, Designs and Patents Act, 1988. All rights reserved. No part of this book may be reproduced, stored in a retrieval system, or transmitted, in any form, or by any means, electronic, mechanical, photocopying, recording or otherwise, without the written permission of the publisher.

Inspire Point Publishing
PO Box 972
Beenleigh, Queensland 4207
Australia
Email: admin@inspirepointpublishing.com

A catalogue record for this book is available from the National Library of Australia

Designed by – Peta Hansford
Illustration – Jo Justino

For Love of Woman
ISBN: 978-0-6482981-3-7

This volume of love poems is dedicated to the special people who have touched my life — and to the wonderful world we might enjoy when love conquers all.

Sing with me ... Sing!
Sing of love – of love
　– for woman
　– for fellow man
　– for life ever after

Table of Contents

Preface	ix
What Right Have I	1
Ode to Encouragement	2
A Tale of Love	5
The Magic's More Than Ever	6
Dare I to Dream of You	8
Sonnet to the Broken Hearted	10
In Memory of You	11
My Valentine	13
Forever Friends	14
At the Death of a Friend	15
Again and Again	17
Our Rendezvous with Fate	18
Birthday Lament	25
The Blessed Brook	30
My Secret Place	31
My Mind Plays Tricks	32
Through Artists Eyes	33
You and I	37
Three Wishes	39
I Dream	41

My Treasure	43
Nothing More	44
Rain	46
The Green Eyed Monster	48
I look – I see	51
How Could I	52
How Could I — Revisited	54
I Come Alive	56
You Are as the Gods	58
But Still I Want Thee More	60
A Private Conversation	61
I Walked Alone	63
Behind My Thin Disguise	65
She Lives a Life of Dreams	66
Pure Love	69
A Lover's Vow	72
I Dream	73
A Woman of Mystery	75
Words of Bitter Strife	78
She Lives at Her Extremes	80
A Certain Kind of Wonderful	82
Whose Name Do You Call	83
The Line Between Pleasure and Pain	84
A Beautiful Mind	85
As Two Become One	87
Night and Day	88

I Tread Carefully	90
Something Worth Keeping	91
How Do You Cope	93
A Poet's Confession	95
About John Saomes	97
Books by John Saomes	99

Preface

As a brief introduction to this volume of poetic verse, I wish to thank those special people who have taught me of love and life; from my parents who gave me life and love, to those who taught me of love sublime.

I believe that life is our greatest gift because it affords us the opportunity to choose how we might enjoy it. Some choose a lower existence than they might. Others feel they have been forced to endure, when really, they have the power to change their circumstances for the better if they would but try.

The theme of this book is simply this:
'A perfect love will conquer all'

What Right Have I

What right have I to speak of love
I — who loved and lost so many times
Scars adorn my human heart
Yet echoes of bliss sing forth
in the depths of my soul

Therefore — I stand qualified
to utter my opinions
My life story — not yet fully acted out
is near its end
I've felt the best and worse
the peaks and troughs of life
This is my story — not thine …
But — by chance — perhaps
your road ahead may be plainer
or a little more familiar
as you share my journey
to see the world through another's eyes

Ode to Encouragement

From deep in my abyss,
I turned my eyes towards the sun
and saw not light nor hope nor meaning,
only more of my despair.
Then there was you.

And from my chasms edge I turned,
to see a sweet enticing path
I might have tread with wanton sighs
to promises of hope.
My hope was you.

And through my faded eyes I gazed
into your heart and felt your warmth.
You charmed the icy tendrils
that were choking my desires.
You gave me life again.

FOR LOVE OF WOMAN

You lighted up my world,
my shining Goddess bathed in gold.
More precious and more perfect
than a thousand rising suns.
You made me see.

And though my cautious hesitations
marred my footsteps, hedged my way,
through endless breathless sojourn,
and wrestling of two minds —
You filled me up.

The scent of secret longing
resurrected old emotions,
and witnessed my awakening
from innocence to deepest love.
You touched my heart.

And now I am because of you
a living, breathing, feeling soul;
who knows of love so heavenly,
and passion, pure, divine.
You made me whole.

JOHN SAOMES

I owe you everything I am.
You touched my heart — you gave me hope.
You are my eternal love.
My every wish. My heart's desire.
Unworthy as I am, I'm blessed.
For you have rescued me.

A Tale of Love

A tale of love I tell for you
- of joy and sorrow
- of pleasure and pain
- of lust and loathing
- fair and foul
- of unholy envy
- of days of wonderment
- of heavenly choirs
- and moments of passion
- and sheer delight

The Magic's More Than Ever

He stumbles sometimes…
'These old legs ain't what they used to be…'
'I used to run the hundred in a flash…'
But now the hundred's ninety-nine too far…
One wilful careful prayerful step —
Pause to take another breath —
to make sure all is right
before he steps out once again.

She forgets things sometimes…
'I know I saw it somewhere…'
'I can't remember where.'
'What's their name? You know the ones.'
'Oh dear… I should remember that…'
The muddled mess gets more and more
    entangled
…new info seeping in and out again —
It mingles with the mix — a brief encounter —
but never seems to find a place to stay…

But — the magic's more than ever
when he looks into her eyes…
sitting — holding hands
and time stands still.
And all the world is perfect
as they tenderly embrace…
and love takes on new meaning
when you see them smiling there

'Life is like a dance' they said…
'We each go round and round,
together doing all we can
to keep from falling down…'
'The trick is found in knowing when
to lead and when to follow…'
For each one in their time and place,
holds the key to wondrous grace
…and shares it with the other…

As for me — I'm young…
but… I'll age without a moment of regret —
for if I find a glimmer
of the love they've found together…
'twill be the greatest treasure —
any human heart could hold…

Dare I to Dream of You

I dreamed a dream of you my love
the sweetest dream a man may dare
a dream so grand and marvellous
but never dreamed it might come true

I've dreamed of you and love and life
of joy so splendid and complete
blessed with every wondrous gift
a dream so high and wide and deep

I dared to dream so many things
in days now past that came to nought
The biggest dreams were dreams of us
but far too grand for mortal minds

This world is full of sin and pain
where dreams so quickly wilt and die
where few can scarcely dream at all
so why am I so unrestrained?

FOR LOVE OF WOMAN

Because I chanced to meet an Angel
one so wonderful and rare
you touched my hand and heart and soul
inspiring dreams of godliness

My Angel makes my life complete
inspires me to victory
fills my breast with majesty
soothes my angry troubled mind

And so I dare to dream again
the kind of dreams that few may dare
You conjure visions of heavenly bliss
The throne of God is mine!

Sonnet to the Broken Hearted

Oh that you could see me now;
a sorry soul who can't forget.
I know you'd surely wonder how
a man could bare such deep regret.

And you? How are you faring now?
Or are you shattered deep inside?
Are you standing tall and proud;
or stooped in agony… as I?

And do you lie awake at night,
and count the sparkling dancing stars;
or sleep and dream as lovers might;
or dress your wounds and count your scars?

You know I only think of you.
Do you think about me too?

In Memory of You

Behind your laughing eyes I saw,
by shadow of the rising moon,
your naked insecurity; and cried,
for I could help you not.

I wish that I were close to you.
Close enough to bear you up,
and share your burdens day by day;
and kiss your cheek each night.

I see you often in my dreams.
We walk together, hand in hand,
and share our deepest secret thoughts.
In perfect harmony we soar.

We spoke of sadness, joy and pain;
and bared our scars and old regrets.
And we were pierced through the heart
by unseen shafts from cupids bow.

JOHN SAOMES

My desperation haunts my sleep.
I want to make you part of me;
and hold you close within my soul;
and kiss your tears away.

Your voice is like the morning due.
Your laughter like a child at play.
Your smile like sunset and sunrise.
Your tender touch a babe's first breath.

I've never loved as I loved you.
I've never known such perfect bliss.
Yet I may never know again
the fleeting promise of your kiss.

My Valentine

How do I love thee?

In more ways than I can begin to recount
    Deeper and more intensely
    than words can express…

    I appreciate you
    I revere you
    I adore you
    I worship you
    I dedicate my all to you

    You are the light in my darkness
    The joy in my soul
    The fire in my eyes
    The tenderness in my touch
    The calm in my voice
    My strength and courage
    My greatest blessing
    The love of my life

Forever Friends

Something secret. Something sacred.
Something special in your eyes;
keeps me restless, keeps me breathless,
keeps me lonely in the night.

Like a spirit through the ages,
like an echo in my mind,
like a whisper in the darkness.
Old friends from another time.

Something tells me we were lovers
in a life we've lived before.
Speaking secret fond forevers
in a world we can't recall.

Mem'ries stealing. Familiar feelings.
Walking different roads through time.
Now and then we're intersecting.
There's no end to you and I.

At the Death of a Friend

I sit on a hill overlooking the world.
The beauty surrounds me, resplendent to view.
But day dawns and night skies and earth's
    seven wonders,
are less than a breath of my memories of you.

For you are more than heaven and earth.
You were my heartbeat — my last gasping breath.
Without you there's nothing of worth
    or of pleasure.
With you, I was living. Without you is death.

Far worse than the death of the silent
    and sleeping,
of those fond departed no more to return.
For my death is living a life without meaning,
a pointless existence with nowhere to turn.

I think of you and the joy and the laughter
and all of the intimate secrets we shared,
of sweet loving gestures and warm tender glances,
and choke with emotion and wish you were here.

And often I stir in the dark before morning
and think of you — aching and full with desire;
and dream of your loving and tender embraces,
emotions entangled… and heavenly choirs.

And often I feel you — arms wrapped around me;
that moment of magic — that touching of hearts.
We clung to each other like two missing pieces
of life's greatest puzzle — both made whole at last.
But I dared not kiss you or touch you with
    passion,
through fear my advances would not be returned,
and in a moment my hopes and longing
be crushed and battered and scattered and burned.

So high on a hill I sit with my mem'ries.
I gaze at the sky. She smiles down at me.
And I'm overcome with the sadness of parting,
and die with regrets of what might have been.

Again and Again

I dreamt of you again last night,
a lover's game of kiss and tell!
Another dream of pure delight,
of holding hands and wishing wells.

By day I try to tell my mind
it mustn't think of you this way.
But in the quiet dark of night,
it simply won't be held at bay!

And so it strays to thoughts of you,
to tender magic moments shared.
And what am I supposed to do?
I close my eyes and you are there!

And we're together once again.
My love for you will never end.

Our Rendezvous with Fate

Years before we met I knew
that you would come along one day;
a sweet seductive temptress
to steal my heart away.

I always vowed I'd shun you,
and not be drawn inside your web;
but I could not anticipate
the promise of such perfect bliss.

Destiny's a curious creature.
Time, the chief controller sways,
and oscillates from good to bad,
from right to wrong, from strong to weak.

You arrived when I was weakest,
sorely wanting something more.
I welcomed you with open arms,
surrendering my burning soul.

FOR LOVE OF WOMAN

You weren't the first to tempt my lust,
and not the last to wave your wand.
But you're the sweetest fruit I've seen,
more perfect than I'd ever hoped.

Surely there could never be
a lady lovelier than you.
Mind so bright and deeply thinking…
…body beautiful and ripe.

We talked of many splendid things.
We entertained such wanton thoughts.
I never ever dared to dream
that any mind was so like mine.

How proud I'd be to escort you.
Out… for all the world to see.
My heart would swell with unmatched joy
that you had chosen me.

Did we drown in base desires?
Did we delve to deepest depths
of private pleasure's sweet excess?
Perhaps… but only in our heads.

But how you'd stimulate my mind
with passion's brilliant icy fire.
The promise was enough and more…
and each encounter took me higher…

…to the pinnacle of pain.
The choices lay before me clear…
the agony of ecstasy…
the brutal blow of broken chains.

Choices often come our way.
We seem to make them every day.
But never have I knelt to pray
so many times… so many days…

For only God could guide a soul
so totally confused as mine.
For only He could know the pain
each choice would surely hold…

My path of reason lost its way.
Destruction's edge not far away;
I wandered through the murky days
with nothing left to do but pray…

FOR LOVE OF WOMAN

But every living soul is cast
a rendezvous with pleasure's path,
to choose his mortal destiny
and fashion his eternal dream.

Fate, the warrior leaves his scars
upon each lonely wanting heart.
And time cannot erase the part
of me that yearns for you.

The pendulum of time has swayed.
The choice was ultimately made.
Eventually we find our way.
What is left for me to say?

Except:

'I think of you each day.'
'I miss you more than I can say.'

One Winter's Day

My Sweetheart fought back tears
as she told me what she'd found
Her voice was sad and angry —
her hands clasped tight together
Her face pale — her heart raced.
She placed the truth before me
And there it lay accusing
and condemning me to die

Inside my mind — a turbulence
— a volcanic eruption
I saw her sadness — felt her sting
— and knew I'd caused her pain
One never means to purposely mislead —
but half truths are like weapons
They have a way of blowing up
— destroying trust and love

FOR LOVE OF WOMAN

My remembrances were not
as they really should have been
It was so long ago —
but that's no consolation
There can be no excuses
when truth's laid bare and glaring
The evidence tells the story
— and no one can deny

I sat in awkward silence
as she pressed her heartfelt anger
It wasn't as I remembered
— but that's beside the point
When you're wrong — you're wrong.
That's just the way it is.
What's left to say?
I felt her words like daggers
and hung my head in shame

My words had not been accurate.
And yet — to me they almost were
I meant each one sincerely — yet —
I chose to stretch the truth
And though I don't remember
the face of who or why
I know with true sincerity
that every word seemed real

And now — the aftermath hangs cold
— like a dark cloud over my head
And tightens around my chest
like a noose around my neck
A slight exaggeration
had become a boldfaced lie
Still — I struggle
with the pure reality of how it now appears

Regret is the destroyer of souls they say.
It eats away relentlessly inside
And no one knows the pain
from the invisible scars that never heal
Eventually the hollowed heart bursts
and the sacred breath of life departs
In the end nothing remains
except a thin skin that veils the emptiness

…and silence fills the endless void
that now exists between us

Birthday Lament

Your birthday came and went…
and I with mixed emotion
let it pass without a mention.
I wanted to send flowers and a card,
to let you know I love you
and I never could forget you.
Your birthday is a special day to me.

I paced the floor that Monday,
hoping somehow someday,
I'd have the chance to tell you how I feel.
The hole in my existence
is an empty lonely witness
to the love I hold and cannot give away.

The love I hold for you is yours alone…
A special love so precious,
not covetous or jealous,
but warm and tender.

Gentle like a fire's golden flame.
A love that's hot and burning,
hypnotic and consuming.
The kind of love that few have ever known.

And what am I to do?
I've so much love for you.
My days and nights are filled
with hopes and dreams
of you and I Birthday Lament
Your birthday came and went…
and I with mixed emotion
let it pass without a mention.
I wanted to send flowers and a card,
to let you know I love you
and I never could forget you.
Your birthday is a special day to me.

I paced the floor that Monday,
hoping somehow someday,
I'd have the chance to tell you how I feel.
The hole in my existence
is an empty lonely witness
to the love I hold and cannot give away.

FOR LOVE OF WOMAN

The love I hold for you is yours alone…
A special love so precious,
not covetous or jealous,
but warm and tender.
together;
and it hurts me to remember
that your birthday came and went
without a word.

I See Your Silhouette

I hold a memory of you,
hiding meekly in the shadows,
silhouetted by the moon,
peering out your bedroom window.

How I longed to see you there,
to warm this lowly passerby.
What joy to catch your silhouette!
I gasped and choked and almost cried!

How can love be so absurd
to treat a lover such as this?
And how can I now face the world
without the memory of your kiss?

Your silhouette like ageing wine
eludes the fading hands of time.

The Love I Offer You

Have you ever really been in love?
Have you ever wished on stars above
for loving gestures you alone could know;
and prayed to God above to make it so?

Have you felt so insecure
and cried aloud for love so warm and pure?
Have you felt the need to touch and hold
a loving hand to calm your hungry soul?

Have you ever burned inside,
consumed in fires of passion's tide,
lost in love and all adrift,
tossed & drowned in loves most perfect bliss?

Have you ever known a love so true,
the sweet eternal love I offer you?

The Blessed Brook

A brook flows by your window,
a little trickling watercourse
of no significance to man;
but oh how blest it is.

For all the sweet green valleys
and all of nature's dancing hues
never were as lovely
as a fleeting glimpse of you.

Oh that I could be that brook,
to lay in wait around your door,
and meet each morning mesmerised
with one more look at you.

Oh the things a man could do
with one more look at you!

My Secret Place

Today I found a secret place,
a sacred grove where lovers dare
to lay in nature's sweet embrace,
and pictured you beside me there;

and dreamed of pleasures we might taste,
of private games and luscious lies.
Forbidden fruits at Eden's gate
where you and I would often hide.

A place where we could bare our souls
and share each other's secret thoughts
and let our sacred love unfold
with whispered words and hushed retorts.

Hidden up in mortal bliss;
I dream again of your sweet kiss.

My Mind Plays Tricks

I caught a glimpse of you last night,
a fleeting shadow in the crowd.
My heart stood still with sudden fright.
I gasped and cried your name aloud.

I pushed my way to find you there.
In close pursuit I sought you out.
In breathless chase through silent stares
I searched, but you would not be found.

Or was I dreaming yet again?
Was it really you I saw,
or just a flash inside my mind,
born of hope and nothing more?

I see you almost everywhere;
but you are never really there!

Through Artists Eyes

If I were an artist
I'd paint my happiness

What colours might depict the warmth in your
 eyes
or the mirth in your laughing voice
What shades show your compassion
or the sadness you hide as you comfort me
Is there a canvas large enough
to exhibit the joy in my heart

When I'm lost in the moment you find me
You always paint me brighter than I am
Could any eye be so astute or any brush so fine
to capture and express the intricacies of our love
What hues could portray the pensive nature
of secrets we share as you enthral me

We take a pencil and quickly sketch our future
We each choose colours but they don't always blend
We stretch our imaginations and peel back our emotions
looking for softer shades and tempered textures
Like young lovers we embrace each other
as we pore over our patchwork pallet

We point to pains and problems
Broad strokes of the artist's brush
Heavy earthy blotches of unresolved feelings
Grey shadows around the edges hide the naked truth
I appreciate that you gloss over my mercurial moods
and don't presume to paint me into corners

Sometimes you want to forge ahead
in daring splashes of bold and brilliant colour
while I become lost in monochrome detail
What colour does that make me in your eyes
What shade of acceptance should I paint myself

FOR LOVE OF WOMAN

At times we stand at different ends of the rainbow
Colours stretch before us,
but they don't match our conversation

Sometimes — if I tried to paint you
I wouldn't know where to begin
My hand would tremble — I couldn't hold the brush
Sometimes it's because I feel so much love
Other times I don't know how I feel
a messy mosaic of anger and fear,
of frustration or uncertainty

In darker times — the colours disappear
and fade to shades of grey
We go from day to day through bland austere surroundings
like ghostly portraits from the far side of the moon
We turn to instinct —
ever conscious of our thoughts and recollections
The shape and form of our togetherness are not the same

And how would I paint me
Which features would I highlight
and what would I hide or paint over
The closer I get to you, the harder it is to see
   who I am
At times I worry that if you painted me
I might not recognise my own portrait
For such is the picture of love

You and I

Somewhere in the night
in the space 'tween darkness and dawn
comes a ray of light
the faintest distant glow
New birth — as the world comes alive
to usher in another day
of boundless possibilities
and endless opportunities

Somewhere through our lives
the space 'tween you and I
narrowed as we came together
And like that first ray of light
like that faintest glow of sunshine
a relationship was born
of boundless possibilities
and endless opportunities

Somewhere through our days
in the space 'tween joy and sorrow
we live our lives as lovers and friends
in peace and contentment together
And each new day brings growth
and steadily we enlarge our scope
of boundless possibilities
and endless opportunities.

Somewhere through the days ahead
in the space 'tween birth and death
we'll move in our allotted time
from early dawn to evening's light
from tenuous beginning to our certain end
And one of us shall go ahead
the other shall be left alone
with limited possibilities
and lesser opportunities

But somewhere through the mists of time
in the space 'tween death and life
I may meet you there again
my precious sweet forever friend
And in the vast eternal realms
together we may yet to dwell
and love may lead us onward
to boundless possibilities
and endless opportunities

Three Wishes

I wish that I might be
the one you long to see,
snuggled up beside you
as you lay your head to sleep.

And as you rise to greet the day,
so humbly I kneel to pray
that I may be the one
who comforts you.

I wish that I might stand
beside you hand in hand,
and be the one you choose
to have and hold.

And through each passing day,
as we make our way,
that I would know
your love for me is true.

JOHN SAOMES

I wish that I might feel
that what we have is real,
and come to know that
this is not a dream.

For dreams come by the score,
and dreamers even more,
but finding something real
is rare indeed.

I wish, I hope, I pray.
What more can I say,
except: my every wish
I wish of you.

I Dream

I dream…
of strange encounters
with faces unfamiliar
in places that perhaps exist…
but then again… who knows?
I don't remember much when I awake

Except for you…
My dreams of you are real!
So real that I can feel your hand
and smell your sweet aroma on my pillow
My nostrils swell with every breath
The perfume that is you will comfort me…
until I dream again

I greet the day intoxicated…
filled to overflowing with your warmth,
your smile, your laughing eyes…

The echo of your soothing voice
rings gently in my ears
and bounces around inside my head,
and chases out the devils there
who goad my longing heart

The sight of you…
The sound of you…
The tender warm embrace of you
keeps me going forward
through another lonely day
till night comes…
and again I'll dream of you

My Treasure

Sometimes the thought of you brings tears to
   my eyes
When I think of the meaning you've given my
   life.
You're the passion and purpose for all I've
   achieved.
You've given me reason and strength to believe.

You are my rainbow. You colour my life.
You are my sunshine. You've blessed me with
   light.
You are my fountain that never runs dry.
You're my inspiration, my courage to try.

I love you so much, more than words can say,
For you are my treasure,
My night, and my day.

Nothing More

When I found you
I was but alone
Empty…
In need of nourishment
Without substance
Lost…
Without a home
Without joy

You gave me life…
for by your tender touch
I was born anew,
and all my dreams came true,
for I found meaning…
for I was lifted up…
and my withered soul enlarged,
and I was whole at last.

FOR LOVE OF WOMAN

For in your eyes I found love…
and joy beyond words…
and endless possibilities…
And though we sometimes slip and slide
and stumble now and then,
I am complete…
I want for nothing more

Rain

It rained last night…

I snuggled up in bed and thought of you…
snuggling too…
The rain affects both of us the same…
And each and every time it rains
I hear the soft and mellow strains
of teardrops on the window pane;
and think of all the tears
that have fallen from your eyes…
and mine well up and I'm overcome
with sadness and regret…

and yet…

I hug my pillow tight,
and somehow through the night,
you come and snuggle up to me…
and I am free…
to soar to highest heights of ecstasy…
as we snuggle close together
and listen to the rain…

The Green Eyed Monster

Jealousy is new to me.
I've never felt before,
that sullen insecurity
that thoughts of you implore.

I've never felt so fragile,
resentful or unkind,
as fleeting thoughts of yesterdays
gnaw away inside.

Such maladies — such tragedies
haunt my jealous mind.
Why do I give way to them,
to frown and fret and pine?

Envy is a common song
most mortals often sing.
I know it well. It visits oft'
in oh so many things.

> I envied those who'd found true love,
> until I married you —
> but with my envy laid to rest,
> my jealousy shows through.

I often marvel at how we crave something enviously until we have it for ourselves — but then we experience greater and more powerful emotions — sometimes to such a degree that we feel less happy because of what we've acquired; which proves the old saying, 'Be careful what you wish for'.

Jealousy is a far greater emotion than envy. But would I prefer to go back to a time when love was a lesser feeling and swap the occasional pang of jealousy for the envy I once knew? A definitive no!

Alfred Lord Tennyson proposed :
Tis better to have loved and lost
Than never to have loved at all

But I'm not entirely sure he was correct. Perhaps the outcome has more to do with how we loved, because love is not a quantitatively definable item, so one love can be very different to another.

I would further propose that once we've known perfect love, to lose it would be akin to being sentenced to live a lesser life; whereas if we'd never known such wondrous perfection— we wouldn't have any real idea what we were missing out on, and would thus be in a better condition, proving the old saying that 'ignorance is bliss'.

I look – I see

I look into your eyes and see
the wonder that is you,
and stand amazed and breathless,
bathed in love anew.

I look into your heart and feel
the happiness you share,
sweet tenderness and purity,
and hope so rich and rare.

I look into your mind and know
your thoughts of many splendid things,
of appetites and passions,
and beauty borne on angel's wings.

I look into your sacred soul
and cause myself to cry,
o'ercome with raw emotion
that you care for such as I.

How Could I

I tried to forget you…
It was my intention…
But how can I wipe away
all that we shared?
How can I jettison
someone so perfect,
and cast you aside
and pretend not to care?

I tried to forget you…
It was my intention
to give all my love
to my children alone.
But only you know
of my deepest emotions,
and understand
my passion and lust.

FOR LOVE OF WOMAN

I tried to forget you…
It was my intention…
But nothing can shake you
adrift from my mind.
For you hold the key
to my heart and my future.
How can I make you
a part of my life?

I tried to forget you…
It was my intention…
But how can I wipe away
all that we shared?
How can I jettison
someone so perfect,
and cast you aside
and pretend not to care?

How Could I — Revisited

Oh how I could love you
if I had the chance.
My delicate rose.
My angel of joy.
My own perfect princess.
The jewel of my crown.
My sweet glimpse of Heaven.
My Goddess. My life.

Oh how I could love you
if you would but let me.
I'd sacrifice all I have
just for you.
I'd give you my heart.
I'd give you my soul.
I'd dedicate my every effort
to you.

FOR LOVE OF WOMAN

Oh how I could love you
if you would forgive me,
and open your heart to my longing embrace.
We've shared something sacred.
We're bonded together.
No power on earth can tear us apart.

Oh how I could love you
if you would allow me,
to hold you and kiss you
and touch you within.
Our passion would know
no bounds and no limits.
Our intimate pleasures
could not be restrained.

Oh how I could love you,
now and forever.
I'm driven to madness
by my desires.
You're all I think of
and all that I dream of.
I long for your love
and your tender embrace.

I Come Alive

I come alive
when I hear your name.
While I survive,
I will say this plain.
You set me free
and see me through,
and I give thanks
for such as you.

You challenge me
to right my wrong
and find the place
that I belong
and stand beside you
tall and strong
and hand in hand
we go along.

FOR LOVE OF WOMAN

You fill me up
and keep me right
and spur me on
to higher heights.
You give me breath
and hope and life
My strength — my power,
my friend — my wife.

You Are as the Gods

As I contemplate your beauty
I feel less than qualified to judge
For I am sorely mortal
and you are as the Gods
Your presence has power beyond my
reckoning

You are as a precious pearl
alone upon a lonely beach
shining through the cosmos
giving your wondrous light
to make the whole universe brighter

Your lustre and radiance set you apart
There are none who can match you
None feel worthy to approach you
lest they see themselves as lesser beings
and weep at their unworthiness

FOR LOVE OF WOMAN

I feel to bow before your feet
prostrate myself on holy ground
but you reach out your tender hand
and draw me to your side
and I am lifted up

And so we stand above the world
like Gods on high I look about
and see the meagre grovelling world
the place that I was once a part
and I give thanks

Oh that every mortal man
could touch a sacred hallowed hand
that lifts him to his throne above
and fills his hollow heart
with love

But Still I Want Thee More

Oh what mortal pleasures
I have conjured up with thee
for I have had the best of you
but still I want thee more
What pain I've felt
near unto death
For so it is with woman and man
Each one so filled with promise
But few there are
whose worth is more than nought
But thou art surely one
of the pure and precious ones
descended from Heaven
to bless this cruel world
with a kiss of life and love

A Private Conversation

'Hello Sunshine!'
'I missed you today.'
(Oh that she could know
how much I missed her!
A whole day has passed away
and I've so much to say…)

'How are you? Fine?'
(How fine she is!
Fine of features and of mind.
I want to feel her every feeling.
But careful! Mustn't cross her private line…)

'How was your day?'
(What a silly thing to say!
Any day that she was part of
had to be a better day
for all who chanced to pass her way…)

'And did you miss me too?'
(My ego showing through!
Oh shallow man that I am!
In my defence…
her love is all that really matters.
Without her precious love
what would I do?)

'Me? Oh I'm OK.'
(Now! Her healing voice
keeps my many miseries at bay.
But every day is a lonely day
without her…)

'I wish you were here…
or I were there…'
(One day… maybe one day…)

I Walked Alone

I walked alone…
for you were gone…
and I was sad — and on my own
unsettled by the thought
that hours would pass and die
before your planned return.

I walked alone…
into the world…
in timid steps — and thought I heard
your voice calling after me…
I stopped and turned…
then turned again from my imagining.

I walked alone…
along a path…
to who knows where — with longing heart.

JOHN SAOMES

I missed you so…
I wandered free…
without a care to who knows where.

I walked alone…
beside the sea…
where lovers played — and such as me
passed by unnoticed there.
For who should notice such as I,
aimlessly strolling by and by…

I walked alone…
where flowers bloom…
and carefully picked a bunch for you;
and carried them home
and set them there…
awaiting your return…

I sat alone…
Oh pensive me…
Oh worthless sole — unwittingly
lost to sensibility…
pining she who comforts me…
I wait for your return.

Behind My Thin Disguise

When I cry at night
you aren't aware.
You're fast asleep
without a care.
And I'm alone
and lying there…
with thoughts
too sad to bear.

But come the dawn
I dry my eyes,
another day
of lows and highs…
I live a wretched
life of lies
and hide behind
my thin disguise.

She Lives a Life of Dreams

She lives a life inspired of aberrant dreams
Nothing in her day is difficult — for her
Petty problems never phase her
   ... or trouble her superior mind
   ... or cause unnecessary contention

She's always in control of her emotions
and deals with life's small tragedies
with grace and dignity
   ... while others marvel at her deft capacity
   ... as she quietly makes her way without
      distraction

Everything about her is elegant
Her gestures calm and orderly
Her voice firm and commanding
   ... yet gentle and respectful
   ... soft and reassuring

FOR LOVE OF WOMAN

There is warmth behind her all-seeing eyes
Nothing escapes her sentient attentions
She considers every diminutive detail
… and lets the looming lampoons pass without critique
… never compromised by angst
or swayed by selfish ambition

Most of her contemporaries are daily struggling
Stress and anguish consume their every effort
They watch the clock and worry about schedules
… a mad scurry before their self-imposed deadlines
… a flurry of activity to be ready on time

And after the madness of their workday they falter
and stumble through their nights haphazardly
while by her prudent choosing she is carefully cared for
… ritually locked away from every turbulent threat
… quietly concealed from harm

Her life is uncompromising
She holds fast to her unadulterated existence
She is surrounded by pleasantries
… for such is her tasteful insistence
… She expects the very best and settles for
  nothing less

She sleeps in innocence
in peaceful restful slumber
uninterrupted by dastardly demons
… free from frustration
… unfettered by anguish or regret

Her ambitions are just and uncomplicated
Her world is cleverly organised
Her judgements reflect the wisdom of the
  generations
… her faith in human nature unwavering
… her compassion overwhelming

She lives in love and peacefulness
The Gods of Heaven and Earth attend her
Her choices exalt her
… nature is her friend and ally
… for hers is a life of dreams

Pure Love

My woman completes me
She heals the holes in my understanding
and the cracks in my character
She fills me up to overflowing
and polishes my persona
and keeps me warm inside

She picks up after my untidiness
She finishes my sentences
She speaks for me when I'm speechless
She overlooks my glaring inadequacies
She tolerates my intolerances
She forgives the unforgivable

When dark clouds gather
she shelters me
When I'm racked with pain
she comforts me
When I'm filled with uncertainty
she shows me the way

Yet she stands alone
and asks for nothing
needs nothing
wants nothing from me
for she is complete
of herself

She is as a splendid chef
taking tasteless ingredients
and serving up banquets
turning famines into feasts
Even the crumbs of life with her
are tasty morsels

She causes me to stretch
to aim higher
to be stronger
to see more clearly
She spurs me ever onward to greatness
She inspires me to heavenly perspectives

She is as a fountain
gushing forth pure love
The kind of love that overcomes all
that heals every wound
and forgives every sin
and washes everything clean again

FOR LOVE OF WOMAN

I want to build a throne for her
and place her upon it
and fall at her feet
and worship her
For she is my Queen
and I am nothing in her presence

Because of her
every day is wonderful
every night is a dream come true
every moment is magic
the world is a better place
…and I am a better man

A Lover's Vow

I vow this day
by earth and sky
to never make
my true love cry

I beat myself
a thousand blows
for words I spoke
that hurt her so

For even if
my words were right
nothing justifies
her plight

Fair punishment
would be to die
for making my
sweet angel cry

I Dream

I dream…
of strange encounters
with faces unfamiliar
in places that perhaps exist…
but then again… who knows?
I don't remember much when I awake.

Except for you…
My dreams of you are real!
So real that I can feel your hand
and smell your sweet aroma on my pillow!
My nostrils swell with every breath.
The perfume that is you will comfort me…
until I dream again…

I greet the day intoxicated…
filled to overflowing with your warmth,
your smile, your laughing eyes…
The echo of your soothing voice

rings gently in my ears
and bounces round inside my head;
and chases out the devils there
who goad my longing heart…

The sight of you…
The sound of you…
The tender warm embrace of you…
keeps me going forward
through another lonely day…
till night comes…
and again I'll dream of you.

A Woman of Mystery

Mysterious woman
What must I do
to breach the walls
around your heart…
to conquer your emotions,
to overcome your fears…
to chase away your looming doubt
and keep the devils out?

What thoughts resound
inside your head?
What words would change
your dogged mind?
What desperate pleas
would thaw the cold?
What talk of love
would light your soul?

Mysterious woman
you cause me to ponder,
to struggle and flounder
and gasp for breath.
You hold me helpless
in your hands,
waiting…
for your next request.

At times I want to scream at you,
and boldly tell you how I feel,
and let out my frustrations
to break the choking silence.

Your harsh and horrid tones lash out.
You thrash me with your words,
and leave me bruised and beaten down
and bleeding deep inside.

Your logic seems unbalanced,
twisted and unfair —
your criticisms callous —
assumptions quite untrue.

FOR LOVE OF WOMAN

Yet in the end I blame myself
for causing you to tremble so,
and beat myself a thousand stripes
because of your complaint.

I pray for understanding —
to know how I should be…
while you remain a paradox —
a woman of mystery.

Words of Bitter Strife

I hurt myself today —
My words of bitter strife
struck the pure and tender heart
of my dear precious wife

Words from devil's tongues escaped —
and ne'er were words so harshly spake
I felt her heart to swell and break
and cry at my profound mistake

Oh callous man — what sordid scenes
What harsh insensitivities
Such thoughtless, cold catastrophe
I winced and felt her injury

I stopped myself — I spoke her name
Stunned and wracked with guilt and blame
and trembling, stumbling, filled with shame
that I should cause my true love pain

Now I am wounded through the heart
My pride is bruised and torn apart
I want to make amends but can't
wipe away those rued remarks

Regret consumes a sorry soul
As I relive that selfish scold
I will, through time, as I grow old,
revisit punishments untold

She Lives at Her Extremes

She lives at her extremes…
Everything about her
has an overt sense of excess
She talks too much
She laughs too loud
She can't sit still a moment
more than good manners dictate

She lives at her extremes…
She works too hard — too long
Every effort is the best she has
Every moment is another assault
from her ever growing list of dependents
commanding constant care

FOR LOVE OF WOMAN

She lives at her extremes…
forgives too quickly
and smiles too often
defying the best of human nature
to the respectful applause of others
and the silent sacrifice of her own sanity

She lives at her extremes…
The calamity of her life is overflowing
and all who chance to meet and greet
are drawn into the vacuum she creates
They gasp for breathe at her leaving
exhausted by her intensity

Yet I love her…
for all her strengths and weaknesses
she captivates my heart
I admire her impetuous passion
to live so close to the edge…
to cope amid such wild and windy weather
…and sometimes I wantonly wish
I were more like her than me…

A Certain Kind of Wonderful

There's a certain kind of wonderful,
like sweet perfume, the smell of spring,
that resonates within the walls
and echoes up on down the halls
of home — when baby sings…

Her song is warm and wonderful.
Its sweet refrain like morning dew,
touches and refreshes all,
who chance to hear her angel's call
to nourish and restore with breath anew.

And I feel warm and wonderful,
lifted up to Heaven by her song.
It penetrates the heart of me.
My ears do hear, my eyes do see
her beauty — and I feel to sing along.

Whose Name Do You Call

Whose name do you call
neath the bright moonlight…
when restless sleep
holds your eyes shut tight…
when you're all alone
for none to see —
Do you have a thought of me?

Whose name do you call
in the early morn…
in fleeting dreams
before the dawn…
when visions swell
with sweet red wine —
I know my love it is not mine.

The Line Between Pleasure and Pain

I'm glad you told me…
your secret shared…
I'm pleased for you
that he still cares…

I traced the line between pleasure and pain…
a segmented squiggle etched in my mind…
a disjointed diagram — boundaries blurred…
woven through the corridors of time…

A fine line — of vague dimensions…
a hidden path — a narrow way…
It shows itself then disappears…
like the space 'tween night and day…

A Beautiful Mind

'You have a beautiful mind,' she said
Her words came like a sweet caress —
like the touch of morning on a frozen lake —
like sunset over a parched and lifeless desert

I smiled…
but words would not be found to answer

We parted then…
I walked away —
my heart pounding somewhere deep inside
like jungle drums
brought to life by a thousand beating hands

…and to this day I remember her words
and ponder their significance
to one so in need of love
…so wanting of affection
…and I remember still that feeling
that someone found something of me
so worthy of praise

As Two Become One

Each night I lie in bed beside you,
filled with longing heartfelt love.
I want to wrap myself around you
in perfect contentment — as two become one.

But life hasn't dealt us the hand of perfection,
and we must be happy with less than we might;
and dream of the day when all will be better;
and work for the good times to put things aright.

For we can become eternal companions,
but we both together must walk hand in hand,
and work out the faults and failings between us.
In time comes perfection, for woman and man.

So onward we go down the road to refinement,
attacking the problems, and not you or I.
For life is for living and loving and learning;
and perfect happiness comes — by and by.

Night and Day

Another night and day,
another wondrous stay,
as I kneel down to pray,
I've so much to say:

I give thanks for you,
and all you say and do,
and how you love me true,
and fill my soul anew.

Your passion fills me up
and overflows my cup,
I feast, I gorge, I sup,
my senses sweet erupt.

Another day and night.
I sometimes think I might
change my wrongs to right,
and face the morning bright…

FOR LOVE OF WOMAN

… repentant, cleansed and true,
my sins — though quite a few,
behind me now anew,
and all because of you…

… and I'm a better man,
who knows a better plan,
and confident I can
be better than I am.

I Tread Carefully

I tread carefully…
for if I e'er offend thee —
God would strike me down…
for surely thou art one of His

Something Worth Keeping

I found something worth keeping…
In a world of waste
where people and products are cast aside
having no perceived value,
I found treasure.

My treasure is you…
At an empty time in life
when nothing really mattered,
you smiled a smile that warmed my soul,
and I found interest and joy anew.

You became my oasis…
in a desert devoid of hope,
and daily I drank of your mercy,
and purpose and meaning sprouted anew,
and inspiration gushed forth to fill me up.

And I found 'me'…
Like a dormant seed I lay in wait,
a rustic fledgling babe came forth —
the 'me' I always could have been,
but never was before.

How Do You Cope

Oh wonderful lady,
the light of my life.
How do you cope
with being my wife?

How do you tolerate
all of my ailings?
How do you overlook
so many failings?

My imperfections are many
— you know,
yet day by day
you let them go.

And night after night
as I snore like a train,
you lie there in silence
and never complain.

JOHN SAOMES

If I were you,
how angry I'd be.
How do you tolerate
imperfect me?

A Poet's Confession

The poets words are fanciful —
They speak of love and lusts excess
and depths of passion few possess
in tones that none could hope for…

The poets words are foolishness —
for who but fools could contemplate
or ever hope to approbate
the nonsense they extol…

The poets words are fallacy —
for only in my mind I see
such fanciful felicities
but never thought them real…

The poets words are fraudulent —
They speak of feelings more than real
and never chance to e'er reveal
that nought of it were true…

or so I once believed...
'til I met you...

For from that night the brightest light grew brighter...
The printed page transfigured and transformed...
and all the poets words took on new meaning...
more true and real and right than e'er before...

About John Saomes

John Saomes is an Australian author and poet whose books and novels follow the central theme of 'making the world a better place'. His writings promote thought and discussion about the kind of world we desire most, with emphasis on enhancing human happiness and maximising the human experience.

John lives in the beautiful hinterland of Australia's Gold Coast. He champions global initiatives to promote and uphold personal rights and freedoms, and efforts to build a better and fairer world for all.

To find out more about my poetry, novels, and get Yuwmahn insights into making the world a better place…

Connect with John Saomes online:
www.johnsaomes.com

Books by John Saomes

Poetry
The Days of Dinkum Dodger - Vol 1
The Days of Dinkum Dodger - Vol 2
The Days of Dinkum Dodger - Vol 3

For Love of Woman

From the Yuwmahn Compendium
Journey to Yuwmah
Ten Yuwmahn Beginnings

UPCOMING BOOKS BY JOHN SAOMES

From the Yuwmahn Compendium
Return to Yuwmah
Seven Conversations of Happiness

Poetry
For Love of Fellow Man
For Love of Life

www.ingramcontent.com/pod-product-compliance
Lightning Source LLC
Chambersburg PA
CBHW030302010526
44107CB00053B/1782